Chapter 1

One For Sorrow

Emily edged herself along the branch and leaned forwards. From somewhere, just ahead, she could hear a rustling in the undergrowth. She was hoping that it was the little cat which she'd spied earlier, threading its way between the graves. One of its back paws seemed to be injured and it moved clumsily with a most un-cat-like gait. Convinced that it would never manage to climb the high walls of the old churchyard, Emily decided to rescue it, but it had vanished into thin air.

She listened. There it was again, the soft sound of swishing leaves. Surely it was the cat.

Carefully she lowered herself on to the stout branch below, then dropped to the ground. As she crept to the edge of the trees, she heard the sounds of a funeral procession winding its way slowly across the churchyard. The cat forgotten, Emily watched the mourners gather by a freshly dug grave and heard the familiar voice of the vicar reading the final words of the service.

There was only a handful of mourners and it came as no surprise to Emily to see that Alice, the church sexton, was one of the group. Alice wasn't in her working clothes which probably meant that she was a friend of the deceased. Nearly everyone in the village knew Alice and, although she was almost as old as Great Aunt Bea, she was one of Emily's favourite people. After all, it was Alice who had persuaded Aunt Bea to let Emily keep Digger, the rumbustious stray mongrel which had played such an important part in solving the mystery of the Riddle Stone the previous summer. In solving the riddle of that ancient stone Emily uncovered many secrets and proved herself an ace detective. It was Alice who set her off on a trail of clues in a never-to-be-forgotten hunt for treasure.

Emily checked her watch. It was time for lunch and after that she'd walk Digger. Not wanting to disturb the mourners she decided to cut back through the old churchyard and out of the side entrance which led into Glebe Lane. Avoiding the nettles and brambles as best she could, she began to pick her way through the tangle of undergrowth which was springing up between the ancient graves.

She had only gone a few metres when a strange noise caught her attention. It was something between a sneeze and a cough, and Emily remembered the little cat which she'd been stalking earlier. Perhaps it had a cold – cat flu even – and needed special care.

The noise had come from the direction of a large yew tree a little to her right. Cautiously, she turned and picked her way towards it. The tabby cat was there, she was certain.

When Emily reached the holly bush she stopped. There it was again – a muffled sneeze and then silence. Taking a bag of scraps from her pocket, she carefully selected a morsel of ham to tempt the cat. Then, soundlessly, she crept around the edge of the bush.

The word "puss" died on her lips as Emily glimpsed

the source of the sneezes. She froze, Instead of the expected tabby cat, two dark figures stood hiding in the shadow of the yew tree. They were a boy and a woman, standing huddled together, looking at the scene in the churchyard.

Without a sound, Emily backed off until she was out of sight behind the yew tree. The shock of discovering that she wasn't alone set her heart racing and it was a moment or two before she was calm enough to wonder about the strangers. Of course, the churchyard was open to anyone and they didn't appear to be doing any harm but, all the same, their behaviour seemed very odd. Why were they spying on the funeral? And why were they keeping out of sight?

Curiousity getting the better of her, Emily craned forward and watched to see what would happen. Within a short time the vicar finished the service, the coffin was laid to rest and the mourners began to move away. This was the moment they had been waiting for. As soon as Alice and the others had disappeared from sight, the woman whispered something to the boy, then, stepping from her hiding place, she hurried to the grave side. Rapidly she stooped down and gently laid a posy of flowers on the coffin.

Fascinated, Emily held her breath and watched. A sudden movement at her feet made her start in surprise and she looked down to see the little tabby cat rubbing itself against her legs. Its first meow was soft but, gaining confidence, its second cry sounded loud and insistent. Emily urgently fed it the ham scrap which she was still holding and peered anxiously through the greenery towards the boy, who had turned his head in the direction of the sound. The famished cat consumed the ham in one greedy gulp and yowled for more. As Emily bent down to stroke it she heard the sound of snapping twigs as the boy came to investigate. Not wanting to be caught out spying herself, she picked up the cat and looked around for somewhere to hide. Just ahead of her a massive tombstone, crumbly with age, offered some protection; the carved skull decorating its top grinned encouragement. Emily hesitated.

"Puss, puss," called the boy, creeping nearer.

Clutching the cat firmly to her chest, Emily made a dive for the tombstone. There was a sudden flurry of leaves and she looked up to see a flash of black and white wings rising from the branches above her. With another yowl and a scrabble of claws, the cat leapt from her grasp and shot off into the undergrowth. Emily winced with pain. Bright beads of blood oozed from the dark red scratch which ran down her forearm. Bravely she licked her wound, then peeped out from her hiding place.

The boy was standing a short distance away staring after the retreating cat. Head down, she waited – if he turned round, he'd see her.

"Alex!" called the woman's voice. "Alex, do come here! The magpie spooked me."

The boy hesitated before answering. "Coming, Joy!" He moved away. "Did you see a cat run out of here?"

"Never mind the cat, Alex! It's unlucky to see a single magpie. Let's get out of this place. I can't take any more."

The boy mumbled something that Emily couldn't

quite catch and the voices faded as they went away. She leant against the tombstone and sighed. "Unlucky." Was it unlucky? The magpie had frightened the cat and the scratch stung like anything, but the boy hadn't see her. Unlucky or not, something strange was afoot. Who were these people spying on a funeral? A visit to Alice might answer that, and maybe Alice would know something about the cat.

"Hello! Em. Do come in," said Alice as she opened her kitchen door later that afternoon. "It's a treat to see you again. How's Digger?"

Emily grinned as the eager dog tugged at his lead and wagged his tail madly. "I'm afraid he's muddy. Have you got some paper to clean his paws?"

"Come in and I'll see what I can do."

Slipping off her muddy trainers Emily entered the cottage, all the while keeping a tight grip on Digger's lead. Together, she and Alice dried off the dog before letting him loose, then Alice set the trainers to dry by the stove.

"You go and sit down and I'll see if I can't find a little something to eat."

A few minutes later Alice reappeared with a large tea-tray bearing a jug of lemonade and an enormous chocolate cake.

"Your aunt told me that you were coming back for the holidays, Em," said Alice with a broad smile. "How's life in the town?"

"I like it, thank you, Alice," answered Emily, "but I do miss Abbotsbury... well, sometimes. The new house has got quite a big garden and we live near a park so Digger still gets a lot of exercise. My new school is OK and I've made lots of friends."

"And how's your dad?"

"Fine, thanks. He likes his new job, and he can work flexi-time so he's home quite a lot. And what about you?"

"I'm as right as rain," said Alice. "A bit tired." Her face looked strained. "I took the morning off to go to a funeral."

"Oh," said Emily. "I'm sorry. Was it a friend of yours?"

Alice hesitated. "Well, you might say he was… Old Tom Avis. He used to be the County Bird Recorder and a bit of an amateur artist. He was once quite a character in the village but I've hardly laid eyes on him for the last fifteen years."

"I'm sorry," said Emily again.

Alice smiled. "That's all right, Em. We all have to go sometime. He's at rest now, poor old boy. He was a cranky old devil, though. Stubborn as a mule."

"Did he have any family?"

Alice frowned and picked at the arm of her chair. "Well, yes and no… but let's not talk about Tom. Have some more cake and tell me all about your new home. What do you plan to do while you're in Abbotsbury?"

Emily helped herself to a second piece of chocolate cake then licked her fingers. "I suppose that most of the time I'll be helping Aunt Bea and walking Digger. I do love it here in Abbotsbury, but it's not exactly the centre of the universe."

"Well, you had plenty of excitement last year when you solved the riddle of the stone. If I know you, you'll soon root out something to investigate!"

Emily laughed. "Thanks Alice. I hope you're right. Have you any mysteries to start me off?"

"No, love," chuckled Alice. "I live a pretty quiet life, seeing as I spend most of my time with those that have gone to rest. The sleepers in the churchyard don't give any trouble – it's the living that cause the mischief."

Alice sighed.

"What's the matter, Alice?"

"Nothing, really, Em. Just something you said. You see, I think I came across a small mystery this afternoon."

"Oh! What was that?" asked Emily. "Something exciting?"

"No, not exciting, just puzzling.

"I told you that I went to Tom's funeral this morning. It was a sad affair, just one or two locals, the vicar and myself – Tom was a bit of a recluse, you see. Before he died, he left instructions that there were to be no flowers at his funeral – the money should to go to charity, RSPB and that sort of thing. Well, when I went back later I found a small bunch of forget-me-nots lying on the grave.

"I'm glad that someone remembered him. But it's a mystery to me why whoever it was didn't come to the funeral."

Emily stared at her empty plate. She wasn't sure whether she should tell Alice about what she had seen in the churchyard. After all, she still felt as if she'd been spying. Wetting a finger she picked up a crumb and popped it into her mouth. Maybe it was better to come clean and tell Alice about the woman.

"I saw a stranger in the churchyard..." she began.

"Ha!" cried Alice. "I wondered how long it would take you to meet her!"

Emily stared in surprise.

"She's a pretty little thing but as wild as wild. She's been seen all over the village but I haven't yet discovered where she sleeps. I thought you'd find her soon, Em."

Emily looked blank.

"The little tabby," cried Alice. "You've seen her, haven't you? It's no good pretending, Em. I can read you like a book."

Emily listened while Alice told her all she knew about the little tabby that visited the churchyard. No one in the village had lost a cat and Alice intended to take it into the PDSA in Oldmoor if and when she managed to catch it.

"You're right, I have seen her," confessed Emily. "I even managed to get hold of her and I've got the scars to prove it." She bared the scratch. "I picked up the cat, and then a magpie flew up from its roost and the cat ran off. It frightened the daylights out of both of us."

"Magpies in the churchyard!" said Alice. "Nasty old things. They rob nests, you know, take the eggs and kill the young. One came right into the garden last week. Thursday it was, the day Tom died. My old gran always used to say that if a magpie flew near to a window there'd be a death in the family. Superstitious nonsense, of course, but strange all the same. In a sense, Tom was…" Alice broke off.

"Tom was what, Alice?" urged Emily.

Alice looked distracted. "Interested in birds," she muttered.

"When I asked you whether Mr Avis had a family you said, 'yes and no'. What did you mean?"

Alice got up and began gathering up the tea things. "Oh, I'll tell you about that some other time, Em. I've got to go out now to see the vicar about the new grass cutter. How time flies!

"Now, where's that old dog of yours? I hope he's not chewing anything."

Emily laughed and pointed to Alice's dining table. "He's under the table, sound asleep. And he's a reformed character. Digger gave up chewing things months ago."

They went into the kitchen where Emily slipped on her trainers and put Digger on the lead. "Goodbye then, Alice. Thanks for the lovely cake and the drink. I'll see you soon."

"I hope so, Em. Here you are – take this jar of strawberry jam for your Aunt Bea. Tell her it's a new recipe and I want her honest opinion.

"I hope those shoes of yours are dry, now. Be an angel and pop that damp newspaper into the dustbin on your way out."

Emily assured her that her shoes were quite dry and left. Hanging on to Digger, she crossed Alice's yard to drop the newspaper into the wheely-bin which was standing in the corner. It was no easy task one-handed, with Digger tugging at his lead. Emily lifted the lid and with a jiggle of her wrist tried to shove the paper through the gap. She wasn't quick enough and the bin lid snapped shut, trapping the paper half in and half out. As she tugged it free, Emily read the headline: 'BIRDMAN'S MISSING WILL'.

It was the word 'birdman' which caught Emily's eye. It conjured up a picture of a gimlet-eyed fellow, eagle beaked and wearing a feathered cloak. But as she scanned the feature she quickly saw her mistake. The birdman referred to was none other than old Tom Avis, Alice's 'eccentric' local and one time ornithologist.

With a backward glance towards Alice's cottage window, Emily tore out the page and popped it up the front of her jumper. Then, unable to hold Digger any longer, she set off for home.

It was bedtime before Emily remembered the newspaper article. When she was undressing the cutting fell from its hiding place and fluttered to the floor. The article was short but helped to fill in some of the missing facts.

BIRDMAN'S MISSING WILL

The Last Will and Testament of wealthy ornithologist Thomas Avis has mysteriously vanished from the offices of Oldmoor solicitors, Carrington-Black and Phelps. Mr Avis, who died last week after a long illness, had been living as a virtual recluse and there is some confusion as to who will inherit his estate.

Police are investigating a break-in at the offices of Mr Avis's solicitor. The fact that the office was ransacked but nothing of obvious value was taken suggests that it was the handiwork of vandals. In an act of mindless destruction, young hooligans lit a small fire on the premises and burnt a number of papers among which was Mr Avis's will.

Unless a copy of this is discovered, solicitors may have to revert to an earlier will which, it is rumoured, disinherits Mr Avis's only daughter.

Mr Avis, who held the post of County Bird Recorder for more than fifteen years, has written a number of popular books on British birds.

Locals confirmed that Mr Avis rarely left his home at Peacock Hall where he lived alone except for a relative who had charge of the every-day running of the house.

Emily sighed. What was all this boring stuff about a will? As she switched out the light, Emily thought again about Alice's strange behaviour. It wasn't like Alice to clam up about anything, but she certainly hadn't wanted to talk about Tom Avis.

And then there was Emily's secret – who were the watchers at the funeral? A rich old recluse and a missing will weren't much to go on, but Emily had the feeling that there was a mystery just around the corner, waiting to be solved.

Chapter 2

Two For Joy

The morning dawned bright and sunny so, after breakfast, Emily decided to take Digger for a run on the moor.

Emily loved the moor above Abbotsbury. She often thought that it must be the wildest, most beautiful place on Earth. Her favourite spot was a tiny valley which, in her early years, she had named 'Gruff's Gorge'. The bridge over the stream was made of stone rather than wood, but it still seemed, to the older Emily, that it was just the place for a troll to live.

The north-facing slope of the little valley was tufted with spiky gorse and strewn with rocks, though by late summer the purple heather would soften its harshness. At the top of the slope a tall, dark chimney pointed a warning finger to the sky, marking the place where, long ago, a lead mine had stood, belching its poisonous fumes into the air. Aunt Bea had warned Emily about the mines which honeycombed the moors around Abbotsbury and Emily knew better than to go anywhere near the old workings.

The south face of the valley was greener and softer than the north, dotted here and there with groups of small trees which, every spring, sprouted new leaf in defiance of the chill winds and bitter winters which stunted their growth.

As Emily turned off the moorland road to drop into Gruff's Gorge she heard the clear, sweet notes of a skylark and she remembered with delight that six whole weeks of holiday lay before her.

At the head of the valley, she paused and looked around. Everything was as she remembered it apart from one surprising change. The derelict cottage, which crowned the south facing slope, had been renovated. A line of flapping laundry was waving like a flag of occupation in the summer breeze. As they passed the silent cottage, Digger raced ahead barking with pleasure. At once a pair of squawking magpies rose from the garden wall and flew off, scolding and chattering as they went. Emily started in surprise then, chuckling with relief, she followed the sheep-track down to the stream.

The showers of the previous week had freshened the grass but today the weather was hot. The bright sunshine was more than warm enough to tempt Emily to paddle in the icy waters of the beck.

Downstream Emily found a rocky cove where the edge of the beck was free of the tall reeds which grew so thickly under the bridge and beyond. Sitting on a large flat-topped rock she quickly removed her trainers and socks and placed them safely away from the edge of the stream.

Digger had already taken the plunge and was splashing up and down, barking madly.

Emily stood up and, using the rocks as stepping stones, picked her way towards a large rock near the middle of the stream. Courageously, she dipped both feet into the arctic current, then quickly withdrew them.

The water was far colder than she'd expected. She tried a second time and managed to prolong the moment a fraction longer. On her third attempt she found that she could just about bear the icy numbness by resting her feet on a shallow rock just below the surface.

The beck water was the colour of amber and Emily smiled down at her winter white feet which had taken on the sepia tint of an old photograph.

Digger's urgent barking suddenly caught Emily's attention and she scrambled up on to the rock to see what was going on. All she could make out was his tail waving frantically among the reeds under the bridge. There were plenty of moorhens about, and it was possible that the dog had disturbed a water rat but, whatever it was, he was growing more excited by the minute.

Emily had just opened her mouth to call him off when she closed it again in surprise. She watched in amazement as a clump of reeds detatched itself from the bank under the bridge and began to float downstream towards her.

She nearly ran, then she saw a face peering out at her from the nest of reeds. Emily stared as the strange craft floated towards her. Suddenly there was a terrific rustling and thrashing; first an arm then a leg shot into view, then there was a loud shriek as the reed raft disintegrated and its helmsman disappeared into the stream.

As Emily pulled the bedraggled figure from the water, she saw that, over jeans and a T-shirt, the stranger was wearing the remains of a headress and cloak made from reeds. She was even more surprised

when she recognised, under the grime and greenery, the face of Alex, the boy in the churchyard.

"Thanks," spluttered Alex as he stripped away his camouflage of reeds. "I haven't got the prototype quite right, yet." He shivered then laughed, "I think I need to weave the reeds more carefully so that they stay together. A bit like a bird's nest, you know."

Emily just stared as the boy began to gather together the wreckage of his craft.

"Is that your dog?" he asked. "Who are you, anyway? I'm Alex Chatterjee."

"I know," said Emily, finding her voice at last. "Well, at least I know that your name's Alex. I heard a woman calling to you in the churchyard yesterday."

"You know who I am then?" He sounded puzzled.

"Not really. Just that your name's Alex and you're foreign."

"I've lived abroad," said Alex, defensively, "but I'm not foreign. My father was a British citizen, and so is Joy. My grandfather was Tom Avis."

"Oh," said Emily. "Sorry! I didn't mean anything."

"It's OK," said Alex, "but I don't like it when people make me feel like an outsider."

Emily nodded.

"So, what's your name then?"

"Emily – Emily Knotcutt, and this is Digger."

Alex grinned, but his teeth were chattering. "I must get dry. Come and meet Joy. She'll like you and Digger. We're staying at the holiday cottage, up there." He waved a dripping arm. "As soon as I've changed I'll explain my idea for the reed raft. In fact, you can help if you like. We could have races, once we've worked out how to keep the rafts from falling to bits."

When they arrived at the cottage, they found Alex's mother, Joy, lying in a hammock which was strung between two gnarled apple trees.

"Hi, Joy! Come and meet Emily. Oh, and this is Digger."

Emily stared in surprise as Alex's mum slid from her perch under the leaves. The woman before her bore little resemblance to the black clad figure in the churchyard. Today she was wearing a flame coloured dress which reached to her ankles; her fair hair was drawn back by a large scarf of a startling green, displaying a pair of massive hooped earings which glinted in the sunlight. She's like an exotic fruit, thought Emily.

Joy threw down her magazine and, completely ignoring the soggy state of her son, grasped Emily by both hands and cried, "Welcome! Nice to meet you, Emily. I do hope you are going to be Alex's friend."

Emily blushed as Joy ran on. "Do you come from Abbotsbury or are you on holiday?"

"Both, really," said Emily. "After my mum died, I lived in Abbotsbury with my Aunt Bea, but now I live in Oldmoor with my dad. I'm back for the summer holidays."

"Oh, that's perfect! We aren't sure how long we're staying but I do hope you and Alex will hit it off. It would be splendid for him to have a real friend while we're here." She turned to Alex who stood dripping and grimy in the long grass. "You'll never guess what your horoscope says, Alex!"

Alex squirmed. "Oh, Joy. Leave it out!" he muttered.

"Take no notice of him, Emily," laughed Joy. "He's just an old ostrich – sticking his head in the sand."

"That's Joy's term for a scientific rationalist," said Alex. "Anyone who doesn't believe in good and bad vibes, psychic phenomena or astrology has a closed mind, according to her."

Joy laughed. "Sceptic! You listen to this!" She picked up her magazine and read:

"Aquarians will be in their element this week when they make new friends and influence people. Halcyon days are ahead when a change of heart will pour oil on troubled waters. If you can avoid a mischief maker, who will make waves and try to wreck your plans, life should be plain sailing."

"There," said Joy. "What did I tell you, Alex? Everything's going to work out fine. Now go and dry yourself before you catch your death. I'll make us some herb tea and chat to Emily while you're changing."

Alex grinned wryly and disappeared into the cottage leaving Emily alone with his mum.

"I expect you'd rather have orange juice?"

"Sorry?"

"I said, I expect you would rather have orange juice, than herb tea, I mean." Joy laughed. "Alex loathes it."

"Oh, yes please. Orange juice, please," said Emily politely.

"I'll only be a jiffy then," smiled Joy. "Take a seat."

She gestured towards two rickety deckchairs, then glided into the cottage, her long skirt releasing a cloud of dandelion clocks as it swept across the unmown grass.

Emily sat thinking about the strange pair. What a contrast! Alex was sturdy and round faced with skin the colour of burnt honey, while his mother was as thin as a wraith and ghostly pale. Fancy calling your mother by her first name, thought Emily and, not only that, Alex spoke to her as if she was his kid sister!

Alex was back before his mother. When she appeared, he smiled to see glasses of orange juice where he'd expected the dreaded herb tea.

"Emily saw us in the churchyard," said Alex to his mum. "When she pulled me out of the beck, she knew my name."

Joy's expression changed. "You must think it odd that I should have been spying on my own father's funeral," she said quietly.

Emily shook her head. "I did at the time, but I think I understand now. Alice Carter told me that Mr Avis had cut himself off from his family. Is that why you were hiding?"

"Yes," said Joy. "And we didn't want him to catch sight of us."

Emily looked alarmed.

"Not Gramps," said Alex hastily. "Joy means Cousin Archie. He was at the funeral. He's caused a lot of trouble, you see."

Emily didn't see.

"But Father found him out, before the end!" cried Joy.

"Show her the letter Alex. It came too late but, at least, Father saw his mistake."

"Joy, we can't involve Emily in this," said Alex. "We've only just met her."

"Emily is a very positive person," said Joy. "I can feel her good vibrations. Go on, show her the letter. She's going to be your friend, isn't she?"

Emily smiled at Alex and shrugged encouragement. Despite her embarrassment she was really quite keen to know what was in the letter. Alice had said that old Tom Avis was a 'cranky old devil' and now that she'd met his relatives they only confirmed Alice's judgment.

"Do you want to read it, Emily?" asked Alex.

"Yes, please," said Emily. "I like mysteries. I was curious from the moment I saw you in the churchyard and then I read something about a missing will. Have they found it, yet?"

Alex shook his head. "I'll fetch the letter," he said, "then you can tell us what you think."

Alex returned with the letter and Emily read it.

Dear Joy,

You will be very surprised to receive this letter after the years of silence but I want you to know that I have come to see what a selfish, stubborn old fool I have been. I deeply regret never having seen my grandson, Alex.

I'd like Alex to have my watch – it belonged to your grandfather. Time has stood still for me since you left. I fear I've been misled by the cuckoo in my nest but, I hope, it is not too late to offer you the olive leaf.

Make haste and come soon. I will try to make amends.
Love to you and Alex
Your affectionate Pa

"Sad," said Emily. "You didn't get to see him, then."

"No," said Joy. "He died the day we arrived in England."

"But why didn't you go to the funeral? Officially, I mean."

"The answer to that is in the letter," said Alex. "The 'cuckoo in the nest'! Gramps is referring to Joy's cousin Archibald Shrike. He caused the trouble between her and Grandpa."

"He hardly caused it, Alex, but he did cash in on it."

"It's the same thing, Joy. You said yourself, by persuading Gramps to cut you out of his will, he was able to grab everything for himself. That's what cuckoos do, don't they? They find themselves a well-lined nest, push out the eggs of their foster parents, and make it their own."

He turned to Emily, "We musn't let Archie know that we're on to him. I'm pretty sure that Archie knows something about Gramps' last will. When Joy married Pa, Gramps cut her off without a penny. The new will went missing when his solicitor's office was vandalised. Mr Carrington-Black says that Gramps had a copy but he's probably hidden it. We need to find it before Archie does. If we don't, Archibald Shrike will become the legal owner of Peacock Hall."

Chapter 3

A Cat Among the Pigeons

The next morning, at ten o'clock sharp, Alex was ringing Aunt Bea's doorbell. Emily was ready and waiting.

"Hi! Come in, Alex. Aunt Bea is in the garden," said Emily. "You didn't catch pneumonia then?" She chuckled. "I told Aunt Bea how we met. She'll probably tell you how lucky you were I was there to fish you out of the beck!"

Alex grinned. "Don't exaggerate. It wasn't a rescue!"

"There's gratitude! Oh, by the way, Alex," she lowered her voice, "best not mention that I saw you in the churchyard. Aunt Bea has this thing about me hanging around there."

Alex nodded and followed Emily through the cottage to the garden where Aunt Bea was working.

"Pleased to meet you, Alex," said Bea Cunningham, pulling off her gardening gloves. "Emily tells me that you're Tom Avis' grandson. Are you a keen birder like your grandfather?"

"I'd like to be," said Alex. "I've been living abroad for a while, so although I'm good at spotting cattle egrets and bee-eaters, I'm still learning about British birds."

"Well, I don't think you'll see any cattle egrets round

here," laughed Aunt Bea. "Emily's father is a keen bird watcher. I'm sure he'd be delighted if you could get Emily interested. He's become quite a twitcher lately."

Emily groaned. "Oh, Aunt Bea! I hate that word, 'twitcher'. It makes Dad sound as if he's got a nervous tic!"

Alex laughed. "A twitcher is someone who goes dashing around the countryside after rare birds, isn't he?"

"Or she," said Emily. "But you're right, they are mostly 'he'. They all ring up 'Bird Line' then travel for miles just to try and spot an unusual bird. When I've been out with Dad, I've seen whole flocks of them wearing green macs and carrying telescopes the size of Jodrell Bank. Now *that's* weird!"

"Emily! What exaggeration!" chided Aunt Bea, but she couldn't help laughing at her niece's description. She pulled on her gardening gloves once more. "Now I've got some potting up to do. Then I'm going to pop into the village to buy some stamps. What are you two up to, today?"

Alex looked at Emily and shuffled his feet.

"We're going bird watching. Aren't we Alex?" said Emily with a warning look.

"Oh!" said Aunt Bea. "That's a surprise. Well, watch what you're doing and keep out of that churchyard."

Aunt Bea looked sharply at her niece. "And where, exactly, are you going to watch birds?"

Alex hesitated.

"Just some birdy place," said Emily, quickly. "Come on, Alex. I've packed a couple of cans and some rolls in case we're hungry. I'll just get my bag and Digger's lead, then we'll be off.

"Bye, Aunt Bea. We'll be back this afternoon."

"What's this 'birdy place' we're going to?" asked Alex as they walked Digger through the village. "You just made that up."

"Well... maybe," said Emily, "but if Peacock Hall isn't a 'birdy place', where is? Anyhow, bird watching is the perfect alibi if anyone asks us what we're doing there!"

Peacock Hall stood a short distance outside the village on the road to Little Oxdale. As Emily and Alex passed the churchyard, Alex gave his new friend a sideways look.

"Emily, you know what Joy and I were doing in the churchyard on Monday, but what were you doing? And why doesn't your aunt like you to go in there?"

Emily shrugged, "I sometimes go to be with my mum."

"I thought you said that your mum was dead."

"I did. She's buried in the churchyard. I often go and talk to her."

"But isn't that a bit..." Alex frowned and chewed his lip. "A bit pointless?"

"Not really," said Emily. "I know that she can't answer me but that doesn't matter. I tell her all kinds of things, and it helps me to think.

"Aunt Bea says it's morbid, but it isn't. I like the churchyard. I think it's a lovely place. On Monday I was trying to track down a stray cat that I'd seen."

"Oh, yes, the cat. I remember now. I heard it meowing," said Alex.

"Alice says that it's been seen all over the village but no one seems to know where it comes from."

"Oh yes, you mentioned her before," said Alex. "Who is she?"

"Alice is the church sexton. That's another reason why I like to go into the churchyard. She works there and she's great. I think she knew your grandpa. I'll take you to meet her, if you like. She makes great cakes."

Alex laughed. "Right. I think I'd like that. Joy isn't much into food and her cooking is definitely not what you'd call great. In fact, *I'm* a better cook than Joy is!"

"Why do you call your mother by her first name?" asked Emily. "It sounds odd."

"Why not?" said Alex. "Pa called her Joy, and I've got used to doing it. Anyway, she likes it. She says that being close friends is more important than being close relatives. Look what happened between her and Gramps. For years he wouldn't even speak to her."

"I know, but it's still weird!" muttered Emily.

"Not weird," objected Alex. "Different."

"But you talk about her as if she was some kind of dozy kid."

"She's had quite a difficult life," said Alex, quietly. "I try to look after her and, in her way, she looks after me."

"I see," said Emily. As she spoke, they turned a corner and saw, ahead of them, the gates of Peacock Hall.

"It's all a bit run down, isn't it?" sighed Alex, kicking at a tuft of grass which was pushing its way up through the tarmac in front of the gates. "Joy said that the funeral hearse would probably have been the only car to go in and out of here in years."

Emily peered through the rusting iron of the gates to the overgrown driveway, beyond. "It must have been lovely once," she said. "Look at those." She pointed to two fine bronze peacocks which topped the brick pillars on either side of the gate. "'As proud as a peacock', that's how Alice described your grandpa."

"I expect she's right," said Alex. "Peacock Hall – I used to dream about it, and now I'm here."

"But locked out." Emily gestured towards the stout padlock and chain fastening the gates. "How do we get in?"

"There's a door in the wall," said Alex, "but it was locked when I came with Joy. We had a snoop, the afternoon of the funeral, but we couldn't get in. Cousin Archie has the keys but Joy refuses to speak to him. She reckons that he's had the locks changed on all of the outside gates."

Alex drew an ancient key from his pocket. "This is supposed to fit the kitchen door – if we can only get inside. Joy doesn't know that I've taken it. She told me to keep away from Archie but I'm sure this is our only chance. She says herself that he's probably concealing the new will. He's the only person who'd benefit from such a trick."

"If we can get inside, what do you expect to find, Alex?"

"You read the letter. All that stuff about a 'cuckoo in the nest' shows that he didn't trust Archie. He didn't want Archie to get his hands on the second will.

"Come on. We'll try the side door. I'm certain that Gramps has left me a clue. Joy says that he was always a great one for riddles and puzzles. And the letter was so odd. I'm not sure what we're looking for but I know we'll find something."

Emily and Alex followed the curve of the wall until they came to a small wooden door set into the crumbling brickwork. As Alex had predicted, the door was locked.

"Now what?" asked Alex.

"We'll have to climb over."

"Impossible! That wall must be at least four metres high."

Emily gazed up at the wall. The top of a large holly tree showed itself above the brickwork; a starling settled on a branch then flew over into the grounds. Emily smiled.

"What are you thinking about? Have you got an idea?" asked Alex.

"Not really. It's just that we can't fly over, but I'll bet there's a tree to help us. Come on, let's look."

They walked half way round the boundary and had nearly given up when Emily found what she was looking for: a scrubby hawthorn was growing close to the wall. Digger at her heels, she ran ahead.

"Here, Alex," she called. "This will do. If we can climb up to that bend in the trunk, we'll be able to stand up and pull ourselves on to the wall. There's an apple

tree sticking up on the other side. We might be able to use that to get down.

"We'll have to leave Digger here, though. Stay, Digger. Sit, boy! I'll tie his lead to the trunk. He'll be OK until we get back. He's used to waiting outside the churchyard so he won't mind too much."

As Emily fastened Digger's lead to the trunk of the hawthorn he gave her a look which said he minded very much. His large doggy-brown eyes stared mournfully up at Emily and he gave a little whine.

"Hush, Digger." She patted his head and then climbed after Alex, who was already hoisting himself on to the top of the wall.

"Wait for me." Emily joined Alex and sat staring down into what had once been the vegetable garden of Peacock Hall.

"What a shambles," she whispered.

Sadly, Alex agreed. Weeds were king, but the sorriest sight of all was the broken-down greenhouse which stood to one side of the plot. From shattered panes, green with algae, sprang a tangle of nettles and brambles. The roof sagged precariously, making the whole building look like it might collapse at any time.

"What a shame," sighed Alex. "Joy would hate to see it in this state. She said it used to be beautiful. Come on. Let's explore. We can easily get down from here. I want to find the fountain and the dovecote."

An overgrown rose arch, hung with fragrant yellow blooms and thorny briars, linked the walled vegetable garden to the main grounds of the Hall. On silent feet, Emily and Alex picked their way down tangled paths between neglected flower beds where summer blossoms fought a losing battle with an army of bindweed.

"Judging by the state of this, we aren't likely to run into Archie," said Alex.

Emily looked startled.

"He's supposed to take care of the place," snorted Alex, "but there's not much sign of that."

"Are you sure he is 'the cuckoo in the nest'?" asked Emily.

"Quite sure. Joy says that he was always jealous of her and when she married Pa he grabbed his chance to cause trouble. They ran away together, you see. Joy and Pa. Gramps never forgave her. Well, not until recently."

"I suppose that's what he meant by the 'olive branch,'" said Emily. "It's a symbol of friendship, isn't it?"

"Yes. I think that's what he meant. But doesn't he say 'olive leaf'?"

"Are you sure?"

"Yes, positive," said Alex. "Does it matter? It's the same thing."

"Not quite," said Emily. "I think that it might be the clue that you're looking for."

"What do you mean?"

"Well, an olive leaf makes me think of something else. Have you ever seen a picture of the 'Peace Dove'? You see it all over the place, on cards and things."

"No. I don't think so. What about it?"

"Well, in the Bible story, Noah sends a dove out from

the ark and it comes back with an olive leaf. That's the sign that the flood waters are dropping and there's land ahead. But that's not the point. The important thing is that the dove carries the olive *leaf*. Don't you see? Your Grandpa has made his peace in the form of an olive leaf and that's the clue in the letter. It's obvious. You gave me the answer a minute ago."

Alex pulled a face. "What? I don't know what you're on about. What's all this about doves? You don't mean he's sent a message by carrier pigeon?"

Emily chuckled, "Don't be daft!"

Suddenly the penny dropped and Alex's grin spread from ear to ear. "The dovecote! He's left a message in the dovecote!"

"I reckon," nodded Emily. "Lead the way. All we have to do is find the dovecote and the message will be yours."

Going by instinct, Alex led the way down twisting paths and through leafy archways until they reached a little cobbled courtyard at the rear of the Hall. Three sides of the courtyard were formed by broken-down brick buildings which had once been stables or workshops. The dovecote was attached to the front of the largest building which had once been the coach house but was now crumbling into ruin. Gaping holes showed in the roof, one door drooped dolefully on its hinges and most of the windows were cracked or broken.

The dovecote must once have been very pretty but time and weather had taken their toll. The smart white paint was now grey and peeling, and pieces of the woodwork were broken away. A few bedraggled pigeons flapped around the rows of boxes, feathered squatters which had moved in when the doves moved out.

Emily and Alex stared up at the row of tiny bird-houses which ran in triple tiers along the upper face of the coach house.

"However are we going to get up there?" Emily groaned. "It's far too high."

"We'll look for a ladder" replied Alex. "We can't give up now. This has been a workshop or a garage – perhaps there'll be a ladder somewhere inside."

Alex darted into the coach house and reappeared a few moments later dragging an ancient wooden ladder. A number of rungs were missing, giving it a gapped-tooth look, and in places the wood was split and crumbly.

"It's not safe, Alex," Emily protested.

"It'll be fine. It's our only chance."

Alex leant the ladder against the wall and Emily tested the lower rungs.

"OK," she said. "I'm lighter than you. You hold the ladder and I'll climb up."

Before Alex could object, Emily was half way up the rickety ladder.

"Hang on to it, Alex," she hissed. "I'm going to try the three centre boxes first. They look to be in the best condition.

Emily reached a tentative hand into the first box. "Yuk!" She snatched it out again and shook it in disgust. "Guess what these are full of?" she said.

Alex laughed. "It's supposed to be lucky. Try the next one." He held the ladder steady and waited.

Suddenly a dark shadow fell across the wall in front of Alex and he felt something prod his shoulder. He stood stock still, rigid with fright, holding on to the ladder.

"Emily." The word came from somewhere deep in his throat but it didn't sound like his voice. He turned his head. Yellow talons were pressing into his shoulder. He blinked and looked again; what he had taken for talons were the longest finger nails he had ever seen.

"And what do you think you are doing?" hissed a voice in his ear.

Alex's heart skipped a beat but he didn't turn around. Was it Archie? What could he say? Caught red-handed, he thought, I've blown it.

"Ah, there you are, you naughty cat." It was Emily's voice.

Alex looked up in surprise.

"Ahh!" There was a cry as the ladder swung out of his hands. The next moment Alex was lying on the cobbles with Emily sprawling on top of him.

"Ouch! Can you get off me?" he struggled to sit up. "Are you all right?"

"Yes," groaned Emily. "But the cat's done a runner."

"And that's what you should do," threatened the voice. Alex and Emily looked up to see a pair of pale eyes, set in a face the colour of putty, glaring down at them. They wanted to run but they couldn't; the glittering eyes held them like rabbits in a spotlight.

"Trespassers," said the man. "Probably thieves."

"No!" said Emily. "Not at all. The cat..."

"Shut it! I don't want to hear your excuses."

He lifted the shot-gun which was resting over his right arm and gestured towards an opening between two of the buildings. "On your way. I won't ask you how you got in, but that's the way out. You can unfasten the garden door from the inside. And remember," he tapped his long nails against the gun, "the next time I catch you or your cat in my garden, I won't be afraid to shoot."

Chapter 4

The Butcher Bird

"So *that* was Archie." Emily shuddered. "Ugh! He's dangerous."

Alex closed the garden door and sank down by the roadside. "I'm glad to get out of there. I thought he was going to shoot us." Alex gingerly touched his elbow and winced "I think you've done for my arm, Emily. Did you have to fall on top of me?"

"I didn't exactly have much choice," replied Emily, who also felt a bit bruised.

"This is bad, you know," said Alex. At least Archie didn't know who I was, but we've blown our cover. From now on, he'll be on the look out. And all for nothing. What a wild goose chase!"

Emily grinned. "Stop moaning." She dropped her voice. "Who says it was all for nothing? Let's get out of here; I think he was following us to make sure that we came straight out. He might be listening behind the door. Come on, let's find Digger."

The abandoned dog began barking joyfully as Emily and Alex approached the hawthorn tree for the second time that morning.

"It's all right, boy," soothed Emily as she let him off the leash. "Stop your noise and we'll go walkies." Digger barked even louder.

"I wish Digger had been with us," said Alex. "He would have seen Archie off."

"I'm not so sure," said Emily. "I don't think your cousin was serious about shooting us but I guess he wouldn't worry about firing pot-shots at a dog, especially if it was on his land."

"It's not his land," protested Alex. "It's *our* land and I'm going to prove it."

"Right," said Emily. "Let's put some distance between us and the Hall then we'll have a look at this." She handed Alex a small rusting tobacco tin then wiped her hands on her jeans. "Yuk! Disgusting! It's thick with bird muck."

"Hey! How did you find this?" cried Alex. "You hardly had time to climb the ladder."

He began pulling at the lid.

"Don't open it here, Alex. Let's get off the road first. We'll go into Glebe Meadow and then I can let Digger have a run while we look in the tin."

"How ever did you find it?" echoed Alex.

Emily beamed. "It was in the second nesting box. I grabbed hold of it, then the little cat appeared and gave us the alibi that we needed."

"Do you think that Archie really believed that you were looking for your cat?"

"I think so," said Emily. "He wouldn't have taken so much pleasure in threatening to shoot her if he didn't believe that she belonged to us."

"Is she a her then?" asked Alex.

"Definitely," said Emily. "She's pregnant. But she

risked her skin, showing herself to that trigger-happy maniac."

"Poor thing. I hope Archie doesn't catch her before we do," said Alex. "I wouldn't put anything past him. He's evil. Now I understand why Joy doesn't want Archie to know that we're here, or that we're trying to trace the will."

He picked up a stone and bowled it in a perfect arc down the deserted lane. Digger barked and leaped after the missile, almost pulling Emily off her feet. "Hang on, boy, you nearly had me over! Come on Alex, over the stile. Digger needs a run."

A few minutes later, Emily was slumped under a large oak tree watching Alex prise the lid off the tobacco tin. Despite the rust, he had it open in a jiffy to reveal a small strip of folded paper.

"Read it!" cried Emily. "Quickly, see what it says."

Alex looked at the paper and read the message. "'Your will is my command.' What? Doesn't he mean his will? This must be from Gramps, but what does he mean? Surely it should read 'my will'?"

Emily frowned. "Perhaps he means the new will that he made out to you and Joy – that could be your will. All wills are a kind of command – aren't they?" She sounded doubtful.

Alex shrugged, "Yeah, I suppose…"

"Go on then, open it out," demanded Emily. "What else does it say?"

Alex unfolded the paper and stared at the message. "This doesn't make sense. It must be some kind of riddle."

He passed the paper to Emily who took it and read: "'Behind the peacocks' eyes – inside the maggot pies'. Ugh! That's disgusting," groaned Emily. "You don't think that your Grandpa was a bit..." she tapped her head, "you know – when he wrote this?"

"He wasn't mad, if that's what you mean," snapped Alex.

"Sorry. I don't mean to be rude. It's just that some people do go a little...strange when they grow old."

"Not Gramps," said Alex, firmly. "He had all his marbles right up to the end. The solicitor told Joy that when Gramps last spoke to him, on the telephone, two days before he died, he was perfectly *compos mentis*. That means right in the head; he wasn't in the least bit senile as you're suggesting. He'd phoned the solicitor to ask for news of us. We were on our way back from Nepal at the time. When we arrived in Marseille, his letter was waiting for us.

"And another thing. This tin is beginning to go rusty. I think that he put the message into the dovecote at the same time as he wrote the letter. That was some time at the end of May. According to his solicitor, that's when he made the second will.

"OK, OK!" said Emily. "That settles it, he wasn't barmy – no offence.

"But this," she held up the strip of paper, "is one weird message. 'Peacocks' eyes' – that rings a bell. But 'maggot pies' – yuk!"

"It's enough to put you off your food," agreed Alex. He paused, "Talking of food, did I hear you say that you'd brought some rolls?"

Emily laughed. "You did," she said. "But after putting my hand into those nesting boxes, I don't fancy eating out. I'll tell you what, Alice's cottage isn't far from here. Let's take our picnic there; I can wash my hands and you can meet Alice.

Alice was gardening when Emily and Alex arrived at the cottage. She welcomed them warmly and, after Emily had introduced Alex and washed her hands, all three of them sat out in the sunshine and exchanged news.

"I see you've brought your own fodder!" said Alice, when Emily unwrapped the rolls. "I hope this is no reflection on my cooking."

"I don't think so," said Alex. "Emily has already told me about your delicious chocolate cake."

"Oh, I see. I won't take offence, then. I expect you'd like a slice for afters. Is it the chocolate cake or my company that you're pining for, Em?"

Emily grinned. "I wanted Alex to meet you. I thought you might be able to help him, Alice. You know everyone in the village."

"I see," said Alice. "Well, what's the problem Alex? Who do you want to know about?"

"It's Joy's cousin, Archie," said Alex. "Joy's my mother. I'm sure he's a crook and we're being cheated."

"Joy? Crook? Who's Archie and what's this all about? You'll have to do a little more explaining if I'm to help you," said Alice.

"Do you know anything about Archie, Alice? He works at Peacock Hall. You know, that place your friend

owned. Alex and his mum think that Archie is a con man. They think he's hidden Mr Avis' new will because he's trying to cheat them out of their inheritance."

Alice looked blank.

"Oh," said Emily. "I didn't tell you. Alex is Tom Avis' grandson."

If Emily had wanted to surprise Alice she couldn't have made a better job of it. Alice's jaw dropped open and she stared at Alex as if she was seeing a ghost.

"Tom's boy," she muttered. "Another of the dispossessed."

"What d'you mean, Alice?" asked Emily. "What's dispossessed?"

"It's a sad thing about families, Emily, the way some members are cast out and made outsiders."

Alice turned to Alex. "I read something about a will in the local paper. You say that your cousin Archie is at the bottom of it?"

"Yes," said Alex. "Archibald Shrike. He's Joy's second-cousin twice removed."

"The Butcher Bird!" muttered Alice.

"Of course," said Alex.

Emily sniffed. "What are you talking about?"

"A shrike is also the name of a bird. It's sometimes called the Butcher Bird because it impales its victims on thorn bushes while it goes off hunting for more prey. The thorn bush acts as a larder. Shrikes might be small, but they're vicious predators. Cousin Archie is well named," said Alex.

"How could your grandfather have been so easily

taken in?" said Emily. "It took me two seconds flat to work out that Archie is the nastiest thing on two legs."

"How could Gramps have liked him better than Joy?"

"The Avises are a proud bunch," said Alice. "Your great-great-grandfather didn't name his house Peacock Hall for nothing." Alice shook her head and passed a hand across her eyes as if she were drawing back a veil. "There's something I should ..." she broke off. "Make yourselves comfortable and I'll go and get that chocolate cake."

As Alice rose from the bench and hurried into the house, Alex sent Emily a questioning look. Emily shrugged. "I don't know why she's behaving so strangely," she whispered. "She was acting a bit odd the last time I saw her. I think something must be worrying her."

When Alice returned, she seemed less flustered and very soon she was dishing out generous slabs of chocolate cake and glasses of ice-cold lemonade.

"I've heard stories about that Archie which would make your hair curl," said Alice.

"What are they?" asked Emily.

"Let bygones be bygones," sighed Alice. "Perhaps he's grown up to know better."

"I doubt it!" said Emily. "He was carrying a shotgun when we met him..." Emily glanced at Alex who was sending her warning looks, but it was too late.

"Where did you meet him?" asked Alice. "He doesn't often come into the village."

"Up near the Hall," said Alex, crossing his fingers to

soften the fib. "His hands were covered in blood and his finger nails were long and sharp – like a vulture's talons."

"Good gracious!" exlaimed Alice.

Alex rattled on. "Joy said that Archie was a little beast when he was a lad. He used to hold lighted candles near to snail shells to make the snails come out."

"Alex!" cried Emily turning pale. "That's horrible."

"And that sort of thing is best not spoken of," said Alice. "Mind you, I've no doubt that Archibald Shrike is a bad penny."

"Grandfather learned that too late," said Alex.

"It's never too late, Alex. At least he went to his rest having made his peace. Now tell me about this will and why you think that Cousin Archie is trying to keep it from you."

"I can't be sure, but the evidence seems to add up," said Alex. "When we arrived in England Joy tried to phone Gramps, but it was too late, he'd died that very morning. She spoke to Cousin Archie and he was horrible. He said that Gramps had died of a broken heart because of her and that, out of decency and respect, she shouldn't come to the funeral or go anywhere near Peacock Hall.

"Joy was very upset and rang the family solicitor. Mr Carrington-Black was quite shocked when she told him what Archie had said. He couldn't understand why he had lied to Joy as he must have known that Gramps was trying to make his peace with her and had made a new will.

"It seems obvious to me," continued Alex, "that with us out of the way, Archie is due to inherit everything. Apart from Joy and me, he is the only living relative. I reckon it was Archie who broke into the solicitor's and burned Gramps' will. The second will is missing because he's either hidden it or destroyed it."

"Alex! You mustn't say those things again!"

Again, Alice drew a hand over her eyes as if clearing a mist. "It's like one of those thrillers that you see on telly," she muttered. "All those years that Archie spent lording it up at the Hall must have given him the idea that one day he'd be master there."

"But that's not right," said Alex. "The solicitor told Joy that Archie was paid well for doing very little, but it seems that Gramps didn't like him. He once told Mr Carrington-Black that he provided for Archie because of his debt to Great-Aunt Edith who'd been so kind to him when he was a boy. Joy thinks that Gramps made out his first will to Archie simply to spite her for running away with Pa."

"Nevertheless," said Alice, "if the first will is in Archie's favour and the second will has vanished, he'll inherit everything."

"Hang on," said Emily. "Aren't you forgetting something, Alex? What about the message from your grandpa? Tell Alice about the letter! Doesn't it prove that he's hidden the will from Archie? We found the clue didn't we? Show Alice the riddle. She might have an idea."

"I'd almost forgotten about this," said Alex taking the scrap of paper from his pocket and handing it to Alice.

"Not much of a riddle," said Alice returning the paper. "Where did you find it?"

Alex looked at Emily. "We might as well tell her," said Emily.

Alex explained about his grandfather's letter and how Emily had worked out the clue about the olive leaf and the dove.

"She's a smart girl, our Em," said Alice. "And she's right about Archie. If old Tom realised that Archie was a 'cuckoo in the nest' he'd have made sure that the second will was well out of his grasp."

"But where?" said Alex.

"Is this all you have to go on: 'peacock's eyes and maggot pies'? It's not a lot, is it?" said Alice. "Mind you, Alex, you've got the right one helping you here. Young Em seems to sniff out riddles that nobody else can. The only useful thing that I can think of is that your grandfather used to keep peacocks up at the Hall. You don't know if they're still there, do you?"

Alex shook his head.

"Come on, Alex. We'd better go now. I told Aunt Bea that I'd be back this afternoon," said Emily. "Here, Digger! Come on, boy. Walkies!"

Alice stood up and led the youngsters to the gate. She had a strange look on her face and seemed reluctant to let them go. As they set off down the road with Digger, she called them back. "Why don't you ask your mum if she'd like to come over for tea one day this week, Alex? And Emily, ask Aunt Bea, too. There's something I need to talk about. Say, Thursday at four? Providing that suits your mother."

"Great," said Alex. "Thanks again for the cake and drink. Bye! See you on Thursday."

"Well, you made a good impression," said Emily. "I could tell that Alice liked you."

"I liked her," said Alex"

"You are a dipstick!" teased Emily. "Fancy you forgetting about the clue. While you were talking to Alice, you almost convinced yourself that Archie had destroyed the will and that you and your mum were destined to a life of poverty."

"It's not just the will that matters, Emily," replied Alex. "It's the idea of Gramps being deceived. I've had a marvellous time travelling around with Joy, but we've never had any money. Well, not more than we've needed to eat and keep a roof over our heads. We didn't mind that. But what is most important is that Gramps was sorry about the way he treated Joy and he needed to tell her. We can't let Archie cheat Gramps out of that. Think about it! All the time the old man was dying, Archie was trying to stop him making his peace with Joy."

"I understand, Alex. I was only teasing. I just don't want you to give up the fight. You did go on a bit about the blood on Archie's hands, and your story about the snails was disgusting," said Emily.

"I didn't want Alice to know that we'd been in the grounds of the Hall."

Emily nodded. "Well now she knows, but she won't tell."

"Good. Anyway, Archie had been out shooting and

Gramps would have hated that," said Alex. He didn't approve of murdering wildlife. I wonder who else's blood is on his hands!"

"Oh, Alex, you don't think…?"

"No, not really; Gramps died of a heart attack. But, all the same, Archie is trying to stifle his dying wish. I'm going to stop him, Emily. And you're right, this is the way to do it." He waved the riddle at Emily then slipped it back into his pocket.

"What's the matter?" asked Emily as Alex, began to search frantically through his pockets. "What have you lost?"

"Did I give it to you?"

"Did you give what to me?"

"The key. The key to the Hall. I remember showing it to you when we were in the garden. You said that it looked old."

"Oh, no!" groaned Emily. "Are you sure that you haven't got it? What if Archie's found it? It might have fallen out of your pocket when I fell on top of you."

"I'll have to go back and look."

"What, now?"

Alex hesitated, "No, not now. He'll be on the look out. Tonight. I'll go back, tonight."

Chapter 5

A Mare's Nest

By ten o'clock that evening, Emily was on tenterhooks thinking about Alex. She admired his courage; he was either very brave or completely off his trolley to go into that garden after dark. The thought of Archie lurking in the shadows of a midnight garden made Emily shiver.

She'd explained to Alex why, as much as she'd like to, she just couldn't go with him. It wasn't even about being scared; it wasn't fair on Aunt Bea. She was in charge of Emily during the holiday and she trusted her great-niece.

Alex understood. Joy wasn't like most adults; she didn't much mind about bed times. Alex had resolved to tell her that he was going to stay out late so that he could look for owls. Emily's fake alibi was proving very useful.

Emily sat and thought about the riddle. 'Maggot pies and peacocks' eyes' – how on earth could that load of nonsense help them find where the will was hidden?

"Well, the weather forecast's good," said Aunt Bea, getting up to switch off the television. "The garden could do with a spot of rain."

She yawned and stretched. "It's nice of Alice to ask us all to tea on Thursday."

"Mmm," said Emily.

"I'm looking forward to meeting Joy Avis again, after all these years. She was a lovely girl when she was young. Inclined to be wild, mind you. Fancy, Alex being Tom Avis' grandson! It's a great shame that Tom didn't live to see what a fine lad Alex is... Em!"

"Mmm."

"Emily! You aren't listening to a word I'm saying."

"Sorry, Aunt Bea. Say again."

"Oh, it doesn't matter. How was your day with Alex? I do hope you won't be bored this holiday."

"Oh, no, Aunt Bea, I won't be bored. I had a lovely day. Alex and I walked over to Peacock Hall."

"Tom's place?"

"That's right. Aunt Bea, do you know anything about a man called Archibald Shrike?"

"Huh! A man to be avoided," said Aunt Bea.

"We saw him, this afternoon. He'd been out shooting and his hands were covered in blood."

"Huh!" said Aunt Bea again. "'The secret'st man of blood.' That sounds like him."

"What d'you mean, 'man of blood'?"

"Nothing really. It's a quotation from a play. Your description of Mr Shrike brought it to mind: *'Augurs and'* something *'relations...'* – *'understood relations'* that's it!

"*'Augurs and understood relations have*
(By maggot pies, and choughs, and rooks) brought forth
The secret'st man of blood.'

"That's the one. It comes from a play by William

Shakespeare. Macbeth – it's a very blood-thirsty piece about a general who is told by three witches that he'll become king. Their predictions turn out to be true but not before a lot of innocent people are butchered."

Emily pricked up her ears. "What was that? It sounds like a horror film," she said. "Say the bit about 'maggot pies' again."

Aunt Bea chuckled. "They aren't like meat pies, you know, Emily. Maggot pie is the old English name for a magpie. Augurs were fortune tellers – they foretold the future by studying birds: flight patterns and behaviour. I think they even used to cut them up to examine their insides. A bit like reading tea leaves, I suppose."

"I knew it would be something disgusting!" said Emily.

"What do you mean?"

"Maggot pies!"

"No, Em. I told you, maggot pie is the old name for magpie. There's nothing disgusting about that."

"But what does all that Macbeth stuff mean? You said something about fortune telling."

"Well, Macbeth has killed the king and has had others murdered, and now he is afraid that he'll be found out."

Emily yawned. "Very interesting, Aunt Bea. I might read it, sometime." She yawned again. "I'm shattered. If you don't mind, I'm going to have an early night."

Emily went to her room and lay on her bed. Her mind was racing. She was trying to think clearly but the excitement of being on to something was making her light-headed.

Like any detective she kept a notebook which she now examined. It was fairly empty apart from a list of names, the clue about the olive leaf, and the riddle. She took her pencil and wrote down her thoughts:

Secret'st Man of Blood = ARCHIE? (probably)

Maggot Pies = MAGPIES (This makes sense)

Augurs fortold the future by observing birds.

SO FAR BOTH OF TOM'S CLUES INCLUDE BIRDS

Emily was sure that she had found the link they were looking for. After all, Tom Avis had been a famous ornithologist. But what, exactly, had she to tell Alex? He already suspected Archie and this seemed like further proof. Hadn't Mr Avis described him as a 'cuckoo in the nest'? She added that to the other points in the notebook.

Maggot pies were magpies – that was important. The secret'st man of blood was sinister. She suddenly pictured Archie's blood stained hands and her heart skipped a beat. Was he capable of shooting someone? 'The Butcher Bird' is how Alice had described him. Is that what Tom Avis was trying to tell them?

She slid off the bed. Alex was in danger. She had to warn him but she daren't tell Aunt Bea. It was all too fanciful; her aunt wouldn't believe her. She'd have to risk slipping out of the house and finding Alex. She glanced at Digger who was snoring softly at the foot of her bed. He'd protect her.

She put on her trainers and her warmest jumper then took her large red torch from the bedside cabinet. Lucky she'd bought new batteries! She turned off the light and sat down in the darkness to wait. Aunt Bea was a heavy sleeper. Emily decided to give her half an hour to settle down for the night before slipping out of the house.

The church clock began striking eleven as Emily, with Digger at her heels, closed her aunt's garden gate behind her. It was a perfect summer night without a sign of rain. The weather forecaster had been mistaken. The air was warm and a large yellow moon glowed in a sky glinting with stars. Gazing upwards, it struck Emily as strange that none of the signs of the Zodiac were named after birds. The ancients had recognised, scorpions, fishes and even weighing scales, but no birds. Odd! She would have named the stars differently. She tightened her grip on Digger's lead and hurried off in the direction of Peacock Hall.

The journey through the village was uneventful. There were a few people around but Emily managed to avoid them. As she came out of Thimble Street she spotted PC Brown across the market square, deep in conversation with another man. Rather than risk being seen, she backtracked as far as Peddler's Folly, then slipped down the alley way and across Glebe Meadow without meeting a single soul. Digger, sensing the need for silence, loped along beside her like a great wolf out on the hunt.

By the time the pair reached the deserted lane which led past the Hall, Emily was feeling jumpy. The whole enterprise seemed mad. She hated the idea of climbing the wall in the dark, and the thought of crossing the garden in search of Alex gave her the horrors. Maybe he'd changed his mind and wan't even there! The temptation to turn back was suddenly very strong.

At the Hall gates, Emily left the road and began to

follow the wall, all the while straining to hear sounds of Alex. The ground was rough and overgrown in places, and very soon her hands and face were scratched and smarting. She'd almost decided to stay put and wait for Alex's return when she came to the door in the wall. With a jolt she stopped dead in her tracks. Instead of being locked, the door was standing wide open, inviting her to enter the garden.

For a moment Emily hesitated, but the thought of having Digger by her side was reassuring. She switched off her torch and stepped into the garden.

The moment she was inside the feeling of dread returned. A cloud had appeared from nowhere and was hiding the moon. Emily put out a hand to signal Digger to stay as she hovered, uncertainly, on the threshold. The dog's coat felt rough under her hand but she was comforted. His presence gave her courage. She forced herself to remember the path to the dovecote – it wasn't far. Perhaps she'd find Alex there. For the second time that day she walked this path; earlier she'd been running, now she crept uncertainly like a player in blind man's buff.

The shrouded moon had thrown the garden into darkness, leaving Emily wondering how far down the path she'd come. Digger growled softly and Emily felt his hackles rise as she stroked his back. She stood still and held her breath. The rustle of leaves somewhere ahead of her scared her and she switched on the torch. Rooted to the spot, she raked the pale beam across the dark branches above and beyond her. The light was caught and thrown back by a large pair of yellow eyes fixing her in a malevolent stare. A screech rose in her

throat but a hand blocked it in her mouth. She heard the noise of wings on leaves, then a voice hissed in her ear, "Turn it off! It's only an owl but I think Archie's about."

Alex!

The hand was withdrawn and, gently, Alex drew her to one side of the path, whispering to her to sit. She took a deep breath and released it in a long sigh. "Have you found the key?" Her voice was shaky.

He nodded. "It was in the coach house where I found the ladder."

"Lucky the side door was open," whispered Emily.

"It wasn't. After I climbed the wall, I came straight round and opened it in case I had to make a fast getaway. Then I started looking for the key..." Alex paused, remembering her presence. "What are you doing here anyway? You said you couldn't deceive your auntie."

"I know. It's her fault, really. Well, not fault. She solved the next bit of the clue and I had to warn you. Maggot pies are magpies – more birds – do you see? But that's not all. I think that Archie Shrike is deadly dangerous. Aunt Bea knows these lines from Shakespeare, something about augers and maggot pies, but the worst thing is the bit about a secret man of blood. That's what your grandpa thought of Archie. I think we'd better get out of here. I've changed my mind about him not shooting at people."

"Hang on a minute," said Alex. "Say all that again. Maggot pies are magpies, right?"

Emily nodded.

"We should be able to crack..." The words died on

his lips as a mournful cry rent the air. Digger whimpered in fear.

"What was that?" breathed Emily.

"I-I don't know," said Alex. They listened and the cry came again.

"It's somewhere in the garden," said Alex. "What on earth can it be?"

"I don't know, but it sounds terribly sad. I think we'd better look."

Emily could scarcely believe her own words but now she'd said them there was no going back. Alex stood up, rubbing the wet patch on the seat of his jeans. "I'd forgotten that the grass was wet," he muttered.

"Never mind that," said Emily. "Let's go and see if someone needs our help."

Keeping close together they made their way back to the coach house, then followed a narrow path under rose arches towards the main drive of the house. Despite their dread of spying eyes, they shone their torches to show the way. The light threw grotesque shadows across the path and the neglected bushes sent out spiteful briars which snatched at skin and clothing alike.

As the end of the rose walk came into sight Emily switched off the torch.

"What now?" asked Alex.

"I don't know. Perhaps, we're too late. The crying has stopped."

"Let's just take one look and then we'll go," said Alex.

Like shadows they slid towards the entrance of the

walk and peered out into the deep darkness. The pale shape of the Hall stood out against the blackness, which was dotted here and there with the darker shapes of trees and shrubs. Emily was ready to turn away when the chilling cry again rent the air. As if in response to the ghoulish signal, the cloud shifted and the face of the moon beamed down upon the garden. A few metres away from where they crouched, Emily and Alex saw a group of majestic creatures standing in a tableau. For a second, they were too surprised to take in the sight, then, in sheer relief, together they blurted out the word, "Peacocks!".

The male bird, with tail spread wide, turned his noble head and began strutting in the direction of the rose walk. Digger growled softly, then wagged his tail to show his uncertainty.

"Hush! It's all right, boy," soothed Emily. "Stay!"

"I've read about peacock screams but I've never heard one before. It's blood curdling," whispered Alex.

"Alice mentioned that old Tom kept peacocks but I took no...Alex! I think I've got it! Dad once told me that, when he was out East, some people believed that the pattern on the male birds' tail feathers was unlucky and symbolised the evil-eye. Do you think that's a clue?"

"That's it!" said Alex. "Where do you think the birds are kept? Will they have a pen? Let's look. I'm sure that's got to be what we're searching for."

It took ten minutes of stumbling round the ghostly garden before Emily and Alex came across the broken-down shed which housed the peacocks.

Emily waited with Digger while Alex picked his way among rotting boards and rusting food troughs in search of a clue. After careful scrutiny, a disappointed Alex emerged from the shed. "Here – have a feather. There's nothing in there. We're barking up the wrong tree.

"It's a disgrace," he paused to wipe a slimy trainer against a tussock of grass. "He shouldn't be allowed to keep birds in that mess."

"Let's go home," said Emily. "At least you've found the key."

Keeping a sharp look out for the odious Archie, they quickly made their way out of the garden and walked steadily until they'd reached the end of the lane which led to Aunt Bea's cottage.

"You said something about barking up the wrong tree," said Emily. "Do you think we should be looking for a magpie's nest? Could the will be hidden somewhere like that?"

"I've no idea, Emily," yawned Alex. "I'm too tired to think. For sure, what we discovered tonight was a mare's nest."

"What's that?" said Emily.

"Just what we found," sighed Alex, "and what you can see now – nothing but a load of moonshine. I'll see you tomorrow. Bye, Emily."

Chapter 6

Maggot Pie

The weather forecast was correct after all and Emily woke to the sound of summer rain drumming on her window.

Rain! The little cat would be half drowned if she was forced to go out foraging in this. Emily dragged herself out of bed and stared out of the window. She was determined to save the cat from starvation or, worse, a slug from Archie's gun. She would find the cat even if it meant combing the churchyard and the whole of Abbotsbury. Alex would help her – she was certain of that much.

As it turned out, she was mistaken. Just before lunch time, the doorbell rang and Emily came out of her room to find a bedraggled Alex standing in the hallway wearing a very strange look on his face.

As soon as Aunt Bea was out of earshot, he turned to Emily and whispered, "This afternoon – we've got to take our chance. Can you get away?"

"What do you mean?" asked Emily. "What chance? What are you on about?"

"Our chance to search the Hall! Joy is going to see the solicitor this afternoon. It's about the will. Archie will be there, too. It's the opportunity we need, if we're going to solve the riddle.

"Of course if you're scared or you don't think it's right, I'll do it on my own," added Alex.

"Hang on, Alex. I haven't said anything, yet!" whispered Emily fiercely. "I'm not scared and I think you do have the right to look in your grandpa's house. Although, I expect that it would be wrong to touch anything of his – of Archie's, I mean. But otherwise, why not?"

Alex put his hand on his heart and spoke slowly, "You have my solemn promise, Emily, that I won't touch anything in that house that doesn't belong to Gramps."

"What's this?" said Aunt Bea, coming into the hall. "A secret ceremony or vows of undying friendship?"

"Aunt Bea!" scolded Emily, embarrassed by her aunt.

"Sorry, Em. I'm only teasing! Alex, would you like to stay for lunch?"

Despite his excitement, Alex ate a hearty lunch and, by the time the clearing up was done, Emily was relieved to find that the rain had stopped and the sun was breaking through.

"I hope you're going to walk Digger this afternoon," said Aunt Bea. "He hasn't had a run today, Emily."

"Sure," grinned Emily. "Alex and I will take him out now that the rain has stopped."

"Look at that," said Emily when they'd reached the end of the lane which led to the Hall.

"What?"

Emily pointed to the rainbow which was throwing an

iridescent arch over the house and its circle of trees.

"You know what's supposed to be at the end of every rainbow, don't you?"

"A crock of gold?" scoffed Alex. "A shower is more likely."

"Cheer up, Alex. What's the matter?"

"I don't know. I've got a funny feeling that there's something wrong."

The door in the wall was still unlocked from the previous night which meant that Digger was able to accompany them into the walled garden. Emily kept him on the lead but it took quite a lot of coaxing and pulling to keep him on track and discourage him from investigating too many distracting smells.

When they finally reached the kitchen door, Emily was very glad to relinquish the struggle and tie Digger's lead to the rails of the porch. She commanded the dog to sit then watched, with baited breath, as Alex turned the heavy key in the lock and sent the door swinging open on creaking hinges.

Emily felt her heart skittering with fear as she followed Alex into the house.

Once inside, the youngsters paused and stared around the old-fashioned kitchen. The room was a hotch-potch of dirty dishes and half-eaten meals. Islands of pale green mould floated in the sea of dirty coffee cups which swamped the draining board. Emily made a face at Alex but he didn't react; he was listening intently to the silence of the house. Emily stood for a moment and listened, too. Then she heard it. A soft, persistent buzzing noise was threading the air. As if drawn by a magnet, their eyes were pulled towards the sound; a swarm of blue-bottles were buzzing around the carcass of a rabbit which had been dropped into a plastic bucket next to the sink. Propped up beside it was Archie's gun.

Alex reached out a hand to touch the gun but Emily flashed him a warning look; he turned away and followed her out of the room.

The passage from the kitchen was long and dark but at the far end it opened out into a spacious hall. It was big and bare except for a grandfather clock and a half-round table of white marble. At one end stood the stout front door which was locked and bolted, at the other a broad staircase swept upwards towards a small landing and a window of coloured glass. On the right hand wall, hanging above the table, was a massive gilded mirror, reflecting in its depths the fine, old clock which stood against the opposite wall. The clock had stopped – who knows how long ago? – at precisely twenty-two minutes to one.

Far from the buzz of the swarming blue-bottles, the young detectives felt the silence of the house almost as something solid – as if they could touch it. The walls of the hall were hung with paintings of bright eyed birds and animals, frozen into stillness as if caught in a time trap, waiting for the clock to signal their release.

Emily shivered and felt the goose pimples rise on her bare arms.

"Come on," whispered Alex, crossing the hall. "I want to look in Gramps' den."

Emily realised that Alex knew something about the layout of the house because the door he opened led straight into his grandfather's study. The room was dark, lit only by the dim light which filtered through the shuttered windows. Not wanting to switch on the electric light, Alex took out his pocket torch and signalled to Emily to do the same.

It was like stepping back in time. The room itself seemed to sigh in welcome. Alex smiled and Emily felt her fear evaporate. The room invited exploration: one wall was lined with shelves of books; two others were covered with photographs and pictures, while two large windows took up most of the fourth wall. Dotted here and there around the room were large glass cases containing stuffed birds – feathered ghosts poised for flight.

Emily swung the torch-light across the banks of pictures and stopped at a flash of colour. The photograph which had caught her eye was of a kingfisher, frozen forever upon its perch – saphire, green, orange, white and chestnut – the colours of its plumage were magnificent.

"Look Alex, isn't it lovely?" whispered Emily.

Alex had time for only a glance. He turned to look at the photograph, grunted a "Yes!" and went on searching the large mahogany desk which stood in front of the shuttered windows. The surface of the desk was littered with papers and documents, framed photographs, stones and fossils – the paraphernalia of a life time. Alex picked up a photograph, stared at it then whistled softly. Emily went to look and saw that he was holding a framed snapshot of a woman and a baby. The glass had been broken but, as Emily strained to look, something about the woman's smile told her that it was a younger Joy showing off the infant Alex.

"I expect Archie did that," said Alex setting it upright. "I don't care if he does find out that I've been here. I won't let him squeeze us out. He's nothing but a…"

"Alex…look!"

Alex swung round to see that Emily was shining her torch on a tall vase which stood on a small bureau in the far corner of the room. The vase contained a dozen or so peacock feathers. On the wall above hung a painting of two magpies flying out of a tree.

"'Maggot pies and peacocks' eyes'!" cried Alex. "You've found the answer to the riddle, Emily. The will has got to be here, somewhere." As Alex was speaking he was unlocking the bureau and in another minute had spread the contents – a jumble of books and papers – over the dusty floor.

Carefully, he examined each scrap of paper and every envelope to no avail. "Nothing! I don't believe it. It's beginning to seem like a cruel trick, Emily."

"Keep calm and think!" said Emily. "We haven't much time.

"Say the riddle again: 'Behind the peacocks's eyes – inside the maggot pies'. It's not in that cupboard. Try the picture. Is there anything behind it?"

In less than a minute Alex had retrieved the large brown envelope which had been taped to the reverse of the painting. With trembling fingers he held it out to Emily.

"Look! 'The Last Will and Testament of Thomas Alexander Avis.' This is it! You're brilliant, Emily.

Thanks to you I've found Gramps' will."

"Yes, thanks to you, Emily, all my problems are solved!" squeaked a voice. The room was flooded with light and, before he could stir, the talons which haunted his dreams snatched the precious envelope from Alex's hand and he knew that he'd been defeated.

"You had better stand still or I might have to call the police," said Archie coldly. "They don't take kindly to burglary – especially of the destructive kind." As he spoke he swung the rifle across the surface of the desk and sent everything hurtling to the floor.

With a quick glance he examined the contents of the envelope and then, to Emily's amazement, he tossed it into the waste bin. He stared at Alex, his eyes glittering ominously. "So you're Alex – the grandson and heir. Don't move!" Archie waved the shotgun as Alex stepped forward.

"There's nothing you can do. Just watch the show." Archie opened his hand and showed a mother of pearl cigarette lighter nestling in his palm. His smile was horrible as he leant forwards and carefully set fire to the will.

Emily and Alex watched in an agony of helplessness as the papers were turned to blackened ash. "All gone!" screeched Archie, quickly tipping the ash on to his handkerchief and shoving it into his pocket. "That was good, wasn't it? Shall we do it again?" He refilled the bin with papers and set them alight.

"That should do the trick. If you are foolish enough to tell anyone that I've burned that copy of the will, all they'd need to do is analyse the contents of the bin to find that you were lying. Do you want me to telephone

the police now? They won't believe anything you say. There's no evidence. Young vandals!" He sent the case with the stuffed owl smashing to the floor. "Ruffians! No one is safe in his own home any more."

"This is not your home!" shouted Alex. "It's mine and Joy's."

"Wrong there, toe-rag! It's mine – or it soon will be, when that fool of a solicitor sorts out the muddle. The meeting was postponed until tomorrow so that some old busy-body from the village can attend. No doubt she witnessed the old miser's will and has to be there to verify it. No matter. I'm next of kin; you and your mother are out of it." He patted his pocket and sneered.

"You don't think you'll get away with this?" said Alex.

"Get away with what?" sneered Archie. "All I've done is catch a couple of young villains vandalising my house. If you do go to the police they'll assume that you are the young hooligans who broke into that solicitor's office the other night. Tut, tut! The youth of today!"

Emily stared at the scene before her. The floor was littered with broken glass and papers. In the midst of the mess lay the stuffed owl and Emily moved to rescue the poor creature from its ignominious end. As she stooped to pick it up, a face stared up at her from amongst the debris. The sepia photograph of a stranger held her gaze. The young woman was strangely familiar and Emily's muddled brain thought of Joy – but it wasn't Joy.

"Leave it!" demanded Archie. "He's just as well on a rubbish tip as in a glass prison. Anyway, I don't want any clearing up done. That's the evidence."

"You can't blame us for this! You'd better let us go!" shouted Emily.

"Let you go? I'm not stopping you from going. You're the trespassers. Just be sure to go out the way you came in and take that yapping mongrel with you before I blow its head off!"

"I don't believe it!" panted Emily as they ran for home. "How dare he burn the will in front of our very eyes? It's like we don't matter – we're just kids he can intimidate."

"He's right though," wailed Alex. "Think about it. We'll tell Joy what has happened, but who else is going to believe us? We can't prove anything."

"The solicitor knew about that copy."

"Yes, Emily, but if we can't produce it, it may as well not exist. In fact, thanks to Archie, it *doesn't* exist any longer. Both copies of the second will have been destroyed.

"We've lost the race, Emily. He's too clever and too wicked for us. The first will is in his favour. My great-grandmother died when Gramps was a baby; he never knew her. He was brought up by his Aunt Edith; she was Archie's grandmother. "

Emily got off the stile and turned to Alex. Her face was flushed. "Alex, I've got a funny feeling that I'm on to something important. There's something nagging at me – a missing link but I'm not sure what it is."

"Try to think! What is it?" cried Alex.

Emily closed her eyes and frowned as if forcing an answer to the question. Alex held his breath and waited.

"I can't think. Archie frightened me. My head's in a muddle. And what if he has called the police and accused us of vandalism? What will we do then?"

"I don't know," answered Alex. "It's our word against his. We have to hope that everyone will believe us."

"Well, we'll soon find out," said Emily.

"What do you mean?"

"Look! Over there. In the churchyard! Isn't that your mum talking to Alice?"

Chapter 7

The Phoenix from the Fire

Emily tied Digger to the lychgate and followed Alex into the churchyard. As she drew nearer to Alice and Joy she was surprised to see a third member of the party. Lying contentedly in Joy's arms was the little tabby cat.

The fright with Archie began to fade as Emily talked to Joy about the cat.

"She seemed so timid," said Emily. "How did you catch her, Joy?"

Alex laughed. "Joy could charm the birds from the trees," he said. "She's a magician when it comes to animals."

"Don't mock, Alex," chided his mum. "There is a kind of sympathetic magic involved – animals sense that I'm a friend."

"Are you going to keep the cat?" asked Emily.

"Would you like her?"

"Yes, I would, but I already have Digger so I can't keep a cat."

"Well that settles it," said Joy. "We've got ourselves a moggy, Alex."

"Good," said Alex. "But what are you doing here, rescuing cats? I thought you were seeing the solicitor this morning."

"I was. It was a very short meeting. The new will hasn't turned up, Alex. But, before he read the old will, the solicitor opened a letter from Gramps requesting that Miss Carter should be present at the reading. Another meeting has been re-scheduled for tomorrow."

"It's a waste of time, Joy. Archie burned the second will!" said Alex angrily. "Ask Emily, she saw him do it. You might as well know. We went to Peacock Hall to look for the will, and we found it! Archie caught us. He snatched the will from my hand and burned it while we stood and watched." His voice shaking with frustration, Alex told the whole story.

"The devil!" said Alice. "I thought you looked pale, Em. I should think that you've both had a shock. You'd better come back to the cottage and I'll make a pot of tea.

"I've something to tell you so we can kill two birds with one stone."

Alex frowned and looked at Alice. She laughed nervously. "Pardon the expression! Alex. Old habits die hard. It's not the sort of thing you should say to a young ornithologist."

Emily sniggered.

"You needn't smirk, Emily," snapped Alex. "Two days ago you thought that there were real maggots in maggot pie."

"What are you on about?" said Alice.

"Don't mind Alex," said Joy. "That cup of tea would be very welcome."

As soon as the little group entered Alice's sitting-room, Emily remembered what had been troubling her and knew that Alice was about to supply the missing link. On the sideboard, among ornaments and posies of flowers, was a faded sepia photograph and Emily realised that she had seen it before. Settling herself on the settee, next to Alex, she sat back and waited for the story which she knew Alice was about to tell.

"You may remember, Emily, that the other day I dropped a hint that old Tom was family," began Alice. "Well, this may come as a shock to you, Joy, but Tom Avis was my half brother. It's a well kept secret but it's true. The story is simple enough and not an uncommon one. Tom's mother died when he was a baby. His father, Richard, was a widower. He brought up Tom with the help of his cousin Edith and they did their best by the lad. When Tom was thirteen he was packed off to boarding school and shortly afterwards Edith married and moved away.

"Richard (your great-grandfather, Alex) was lonely. He met a young woman from the village and they fell in love. But tragedy struck. War broke out and, before he and Amy could tie the knot, Richard was sent abroad. He never came back. He was killed in France and Amy Carter never saw him again."

Alice paused and Emily noticed that her strong brown hands were trembling. She smiled at Alex. "Eight months afterwards, I made my entry into this world and my mother left it. She only lived long enough to hold me in her arms before she died."

"Oh, Alice," whispered Emily. "What a sad story.

"Yes, Emily, that it is," said Alice.

"But it has a happy ending." Alice and Alex looked at Emily in surprise.

"What do you mean, Em?"

"Well, don't you see, Alice? You're Alex's great-aunt. I've got Aunt Bea and now Alex has got you. Isn't that lovely?"

Alice blushed and picked at a finger nail. "That really depends on how Joy and Alex feel about it," she said.

Alex grinned shyly. "Emily's right – Aunt Alice. And I know that Joy will agree. It is lovely to have my very own auntie!"

Joy stood up and hugged Alice. "We need someone like you in our lives," she said.

"It's still a secret, you know," said Alice. "Of course, I've told Bea the whole story and I expect there are others who suspect, but no one else in the village knows who my father was. Some might call it a guilty secret but I think Emily was nearer to the truth when she called it a 'sad story'. My old gran brought me up to be a charitable Christian and that's where I stand. Tongues wagged and when I was a little mite I learned what it was to be cast off. Years later, I felt the pain again when Tom turned your mother out because she was marrying a foreigner… Oh, is that the phone ringing, Emily? Would you answer it for me?"

Emily went into the hall and returned to say that a Mr Carrington-Black wanted to speak to Alice. She got up and left the room.

"Well, you two certainly had an adventure this morning. But you realise that it was wrong of you to go into the house," said Joy.

"But it's Gramps' house, not Archie's!"

"That's not the point, Alex. It's Archie's home and

77

Emily and you were trespassing. Nevertheless, I'm going to ring the police. That man had no right to frighten you like that." She paused. "I don't suppose we can get any evidence of Archie burning the will."

"No chance. The will has gone, Joy." Alex told his mum of Archie's trick with the ashes. "They could be scattered to the four winds by now," he added.

"It's our word against his," said Emily.

"You did well to find the will even though no good can come of it."

"What's that you say?"

Something about Alice's voice at the phone made Emily turn in surprise. Her face was deathly pale and she was shaking like a leaf as she hung up.

"Sit down, Alice. Are you all right?" cried Emily with concern.

"Is it bad news?" asked Joy. "Can I get you something?"

Alice passed her hand across her face and shook her head. "No, no. Nothing thank you. It comes as a shock… after all these years."

The room fell silent except for the sound of a clock, relentlessly ticking off the seconds, the building bricks of time.

"It was your solicitor, Joy," said Alice. "As you said, he wants to see me tomorrow. Apparently, he's found something belonging to me among the family's papers." Alice paused and passed a hand across her face. "It's a marriage certificate," she said. "Fancy, all these years I've been Alice Avis and I didn't know it. Richard Avis and Amy Carter were married by special licence the day before your grandfather left for the war. They kept it a secret until they could tell young Tom but events overtook them."

"That's wonderful," said Joy. "I'm very glad, Alice."

"Strange, how things work out," said Alice. "I think this calls for another will burning."

"What?" said Emily. "What do you mean, Alice?"

"Well, tomorrow at the meeting with Joy and the solicitor *and* Mister Archibald Shrike, there's going to be a will burning ceremony."

"Why?" asked Alex.

"The new will, which leaves your grandfather's estate to Joy, has been destroyed. The old will cuts out Joy and leaves everything to the next of kin. Archie thinks that's him but, as it turns out, it's me," said Alice.

"So why burn the will?" asked Alex.

"It's just a gesture to see him off. He'll know then that we've got his number," said Alice with a smile. "Will or no will, I don't want Peacock Hall. According to the terms of the first will, I am Tom's next of kin – not A. Shrike esquire – but, in truth, that really means you and your mum, Alex. I've been Alice Carter for more than half a century and that suits me, fine. Anyway, I've got used to my secret. Like you, Em, I enjoy a bit of mystery in my life."

"Did you hear that, Mum?" whispered Alex. "You can open an animal refuge."

"Well, this family is certainly growing fast," laughed Alice. "You've just called your mother, 'Mum', Alex!"

"I always knew that you were somebody's fairy

godmother, Alice!" cried Emily. "You're magic!"

"And you're a maggoty one, Emily Knotcutt!" chuckled Alice.

"Ugh! Alice what a horrible thing to say."

"I think it's an old fashioned compliment to your imagination," said Joy. "Alice is saying that you're full of fancy, Emily, and that's no bad thing. We've certainly got plenty to thank you for," added Joy. "I don't know where we'd be without that head of yours."

Joy turned to Alice. "You've just made a very generous offer and I'm grateful to you. But Alex and I wouldn't want to take anything away from you, Alice."

"Don't worry about it. You've given me something that I've always wanted – a family.

"There is just one other thing that I'd like from you, Joy."

"What's that Alice? Just say it – anything!"

"I wouldn't mind one of those kittens."

For a moment, a confused look passed from one to the other, and then three pairs of eyes turned to the box under the table to see the little tabby cat industriously licking three tiny balls of damp fur.

Emily rushed over to the tabby with excitement; after all, it was the tabby who had led her to becoming involved in the mystery, and now, with the birth of the kittens, she seemed to be part of the resolution, too. Emily and Alex had solved the problem and now she was going to have a friend to spend the holidays with at Abbotsbury: it looked like the summer would be fun, after all.